The Lamp of Cheerfulness

PATIENCE STRONG

The Lamp
of Cheerfulness

Cheerfulness is like a lamp that radiates
a light — scattering depressing thoughts
and putting fears to flight—generating
happiness wherever felt or heard—with
an optimistic viewpoint or a cheery
word.

Cheerfulness can animate the spirit of a
crowd—something happens as when
sun comes bursting through a cloud ...
Some there are who have this power to
be a medium—for transmitting cheerfulness whenever troubles come, chang-
ing situations when the atmosphere is
tense—lighting lamps that give forth
rays of hope and confidence.

Somebody's Tomorrow

Is anyone the happier for meeting you today?
Has anyone been prayed for just because he
came your way?

Has anyone been helped because you stopped
to lend a hand—spared a little time to listen,
tried to understand?

Has anyone been made to feel that God was
somewhere near? Has someone somewhere been
relieved of worry and of fear? ... Has someone
rediscovered faith in what is good and true—
seen another side to life, another point of view?

If the answer's Yes, then you have earned your
night's repose. If No, your day was wasted,
spent in vain—and at its close—there can be
no satisfaction; not unless you say—that
somebody's tomorrow will be better than today.

Beautiful Moments

I opened wide the window to the morning of the day—and from the wintry branches of the trees across the way—I heard the robins and the thrushes fluting joyously—and it seemed that they were singing specially for me.

I stood and listened. Every note was like a silver bell—and deep inside my heart I knew: I knew that all was well. A word of hope had reached me through the birds ... I can't explain — But that lovely message had not come to me in vain. A thrill of new expectant life along my nerves had run—as, looking up, I felt the warm sweet kisses of the sun.

Happiness Waiting for You

There is light at the end of the tunnel.
There is calm at the end of the storm ...
There is rest at the end of the journey—and a
hearth that is welcome and warm.

There's a star on the top of the mountain—
you can touch when the last crag is scaled.
There's a certain reward for the faithful—at
the point where they think they have failed.

There's a spring at the end of the winter—
and behind the black cloud it is blue ...
There's a song at the heart of your sorrow—
and happiness waiting for you.

How did it Happen?

Violets by the woodland way. Promise
of blossom on the spray. Wonderful
glow of daffodils—underneath the
windowsills—and by the verges of the
lane—primroses beaded with the rain.

Glorious splash of crocus gold—as in
the sun the cups unfold. Thrusting of
tips where frosts still cling. Wonder
of hyacinths opening. Fragrance of
daphne on the breeze. Beautiful pink
of almond trees. Just as if somebody
overnight—had cast a spell and lit a
light—by some act of wizardry. How
did it happen? You tell me.

Take what Comes

Don't expect perfection for you'll never find it here.
This is earth, not heaven, so with charity and cheer—
take what comes, the good, the bad, and don't start
whimpering—when you're disappointed with a person
or a thing.
Do not worship idols and complain when you have
found—feet of clay beneath the robes in which you've

wrapped them round ... Everyone is human. Do not be
too critical—when someone fails. Remember that you,
too, are fallible.
Keep your ideals in your heart and set your standard
high—but don't lose faith when things go wrong. Just
let the storm blow by ... Do not ask too much of life
or reach beyond your range. Accept and learn to live
content with what you cannot change.

The Surrender

I run to grasp the good that life is bringing. My
thoughts leap forward, brooking no delay ... I
come, I come, my eager heart is singing. I come
to claim my blessing for the day.

I fling aside the fetters that impede me—the
doubts and fears that day by day increase—
and rush towards the One who waits to feed me
—with living bread of hope and life and peace
... I run to God—for where else can I go?
What refuge seek? No other Truth I know.

Balanced

Sometimes we walk in the shadows.
Sometimes we bask in the sun. Joys
interchanging with sorrows. That is
how life seems to run.

We can't keep a hold on its treasures. We
snatch at our dreams as they fade—but
taking the pains with the pleasures—
They're just about evenly weighed.

Give your Love

Give your love to others. Don't spend it
on yourself. Give your heart's good
treasure. Don't hoard it on the shelf ...
Give a word of comfort. Give a helping
hand. Give where it is needed. Try to
understand.

Give the best that's in you to the job
you do. Give the world your blessing
and it blesses you ... Give your life to
something that is well worth while.
Give—and never ever forget to give
a smile.

Never Mind, Let it Go

Didn't that wonderful dream come true? Maybe
that one wasn't meant for you. Everything's
planned; though you can't see today—why
things worked out in the wrong kind of way.

Lovely it seemed in the first bright glow. Didn't
it last? Never mind. Let it go ... Learn to
accept what you know you can't change. The
pattern of fate is not yours to arrange ...
Someday you'll laugh at the tears shed by you
—over a dream that could never come true.

As Roses have Thorns

As roses have thorns, so does love have its times
—of testings, frustrations and pains—But what
is is worth if it cannot withstand—the pressures,
the heart-aches and strains?

Love's depths can't be measured by kiss, word
or gift—but by sympathy tender and true; the
will to forbear, to forgive, to forget—and to
take the most generous view—hiding the scars
and the stings that still smart—Ready to laugh
and to make a new start.

Really Happy

Who are the really happy people? They are those
who serve: mothers, clergy, healers, nurses —
those who never swerve—from the beaten track
of duty, doing faithfully—things for others—
and the food of all humanity.

These are the really happy ones, for in their work
they find—Satisfaction which to them means
joy and peace of mind ... Living life for money-
making, pleasure or success—brings no harvest
of content; no lasting happiness.

Flower of the Sun

It came out of a packet, the seed from
which it grew. This glowing golden sunflower
has grown the summer through—and now
stands tall and radiant. The bloom
triumphant towers—shining like a little
sun above the other flowers.

Yet it's nothing grand or rare—A
common sight to see—in any country
garden. And it always seems to be—
unconscious of its splendour as it hangs
there bright and high—thrusting up out
of the earth as if to reach the sky.

Lovely sunflower, come to teach a lesson
to the proud. There you stand in all your
glory with your head unbowed—homely,
unpretentious, yet your beauty draws the
eye—and warms the cockles of the heart
of every passer-by.

Coming or Going?

Do not say you're going through a time
of suffering. Say you're coming through
it. That's a very different thing.
Coming through your trouble to the
brightness round the bend. Coming
through the tunnel to the sunshine
at the end.

Coming through with banners flying,
stronger every day. Coming through,
not going through—with Hope to
lead the way ... Coming through
your difficulties. Coming through your
test—coming through the worst and
yet believing in the best ... No matter
what life does to you—Always say
you're coming through.

The Best in Life

The best and sweetest things in life are
things you cannot buy: the music of
the birds at dawn, the rainbows in the
sky ... The dazzling magic of the stars,
the miracle of light. The precious gifts
of health and strength, of hearing,
speech and sight.

The peace of mind that crowns a busy
life of work well done. A faith in God
that deepends as you face the setting sun ...
The pearl of love, the gems of friendship.
As the years go by—you find the
greatest blessings are the things you
cannot buy.

Happy House

Is this a happy house? Yes. You will know—
once you have stepped inside. Faces will show—
That sort of happiness none can disguise—It's
in the smile of the lips and the eyes.
Is this a happy house? Yes—If Love here—
makes its abiding and dwells year by year ...
Love's quiet presence is sensed and is heard—
in helpfulness, kindness and courteous words.
Is this a happy house? Yes, if so be—somebody
prays in it. Prayer secretly—sweetens and
brightens wherever it's said—and calls down a
blessing on every head.